6/6/6

Team Spirit

THE DALLAS COWBOYS

BY

MARK STEWART

Content Consultant
Jason Aikens
Collections Curator
The Professional Football Hall of Fame

NORWOOD HOUSE PRESS

CHICAGO, ILLINOIS

Norwood House Press
P.O. Box 316598
Chicago, Illinois 60631

For information regarding Norwood House Press, please visit our website at:
www.norwoodhousepress.com or call 866-565-2900.

All photos courtesy AP/Wide World Photos, Inc. except the following:
Topps, Inc. (14, 20, 21 top, 34, 40); Getty (32); Philadelphia Gum Co. (30);
Jim McIsaac/Getty Images (cover image).
Special thanks to Topps, Inc.

Editor: Mike Kennedy
Designer: Ron Jaffe
Project Management: Black Book Partners, LLC.

Special thanks to: Tom Bosworth and Laura Peabody.

LIBRARY OF CONGRESS CATALOGING-IN-PUBLICATION DATA

Stewart, Mark, 1960-
   Dallas Cowboys / by Mark Stewart ; content consultant, Jason Aikens.
     p. cm. -- (Team spirit)
   Summary: "Presents the history, accomplishments and key personalities of
the Dallas Cowboys football team. Includes timelines, quotes, maps, glossary
and websites"--Provided by publisher.
   Includes index.
   ISBN-13: 978-1-59953-004-8 (library edition : alk. paper)
   ISBN-10: 1-59953-004-X (library edition : alk. paper) 1. Dallas Cowboys
(Football team)--Juvenile literature. I. Aikens, Jason. II. Title. III. Series.
   GV956.D3S745 2006
   796.332'64097642812--dc22
                                                        2005034377

Manufactured in the United States of America.
Allen County Public Library

COVER PHOTO: The Dallas Cowboys' front line gets ready to start a play.

Table of Contents

SPORTS WORDS & VOCABULARY WORDS: In this book, you will find many words that are new to you. You may also see familiar words used in new ways. The glossary on page 46 gives the meanings of football words, as well as "everyday" words that have special football meanings. These words appear in **bold type** throughout the book. The glossary on page 47 gives the meanings of vocabulary words that are not related to football. They appear in ***bold italic type*** throughout the book.

Meet the Cowboys

Each team in the **National Football League (NFL)** has its own special *traditions*. Fans of the Dallas Cowboys believe that their team has the most special tradition of all: winning. The Cowboys put the right players at the right positions, and call the right plays at the right time. They pay attention to detail and do all of the little things right. It is no wonder that they have made more trips to the **Super Bowl** than any other team.

When a player joins the Cowboys, he knows that his job is to help the team win. Whether that player is a star or a substitute, he is focused on this goal. In the fourth quarter of a football game, those are the players a coach wants on the field.

This book tells the story of the Cowboys. They are a team of fun-loving athletes, but once game day arrives, they are all business. When football fans watch the Cowboys, they can easily imagine themselves in the Dallas **huddle**. This is one of the reasons why the Cowboys are one of the most popular teams in sports.

Billy Cundiff is surrounded by happy teammates after he kicks a field goal in a 2003 game.

Way Back When

The 1960 season was an exciting one for **professional football** fans. Ten new teams began playing that year. Eight were part of the **American Football League (AFL)**, which was in its first season. Two teams—the Minnesota Vikings and Dallas Cowboys—were added to the NFL.

The Cowboys were owned by a man named Clint Murchison. Murchison loved football, but did not know enough to *assemble* an

NFL team on his own. For this job, he hired Tex Schramm and Gil Brandt. Tom Landry, an assistant coach with the New York Giants, was picked to be the head coach of the Cowboys. During the 1960s and 1970s, these four men would build Dallas into a championship team.

Tex Schramm and Tom Landry, two of the people who built the Cowboys into a winning team.

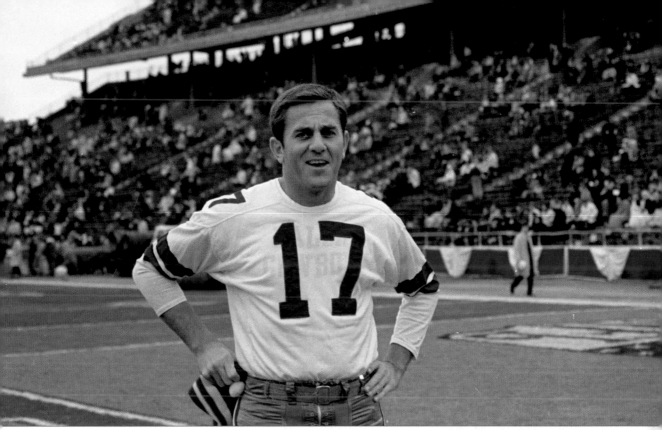

Don Meredith, the quarterback who led the Cowboys during the 1960s.

This did not happen overnight. The Cowboys did not have many good players in their early years. They played the entire 1960 season without winning a single game, and they did not have a winning season until 1966.

By then, Dallas fans had plenty to cheer about. The team had several talented players, including Don Meredith, Don Perkins, Dan Reeves, Bob Hayes, Ralph Neely, Bob Lilly, Jethro Pugh, Chuck Howley, Lee Roy Jordan, and Mel Renfro. These stars helped the Cowboys reach the 1966 and 1967 **NFL Championship** games.

Cowboys fans had to wait until the 1970s before they got to watch their team play in the Super Bowl. Dallas advanced to the big game five times during the **decade**. Landry was still the coach, but a new  group of players now led the team. They included Roger Staubach, Calvin Hill, Drew Pearson, Tony Dorsett, Rayfield Wright, Harvey Martin, Randy White, Ed "Too Tall" Jones, Cliff Harris, and Charlie Waters. The Cowboys had a winning team every year.

After these stars left the NFL, the Cowboys had to rebuild their club. Normally, this takes many years, but Dallas found a "shortcut." They traded their best player, Herschel Walker, and got a group of good, young players in return. The Cowboys also made three brilliant **draft picks**: Michael Irvin, Troy Aikman, and Emmitt Smith. These stars helped the team return to the Super Bowl three times during the 1990s—and continue their winning tradition.

TOP: Roger Staubach and Tom Landry talk football.
LEFT: Troy Aikman hands off to Emmitt Smith.

The Team Today

The Cowboys have played the same style of proud, powerful football for more than 40 years. When you wear a Dallas uniform, this is what is expected of you. The defense is the key to the team's success. When the Dallas defense is playing well, it forces opponents into trying risky plays. That is when the Cowboys really go on the attack—**sacking** the quarterback and **intercepting** passes.

The Dallas offense also likes to win by making the "big play." Just when it seems the other team has stopped them, the Cowboys plow through the line for a long run, or **complete** a beautiful touchdown pass. When the team is playing at its best, it reminds fans of the Super Bowl champions of the past.

Today's Cowboys have good young players mixed in with experienced *veterans*. This is a formula that worked well before. Who knows—a new Dallas *dynasty* may be just around the corner!

Running back Julius Jones gets a big hug from lineman Andre Gurode after a Dallas touchdown.

11

Home Turf

The Cowboys play in Texas Stadium. It is a beautiful field located in the city of Irving, just a few minutes outside Dallas. The team moved there in 1971, after playing many years at the Cotton Bowl in Dallas. The Cowboys plan to move into a new stadium in 2009.

Texas Stadium may be the best known field in the NFL. The stadium's roof has a large oval opening right above the playing field. It lets the sun shine through, but also gives the crowd protection when it rains.

TEXAS STADIUM BY THE NUMBERS

- *There are 65,675 seats in Texas Stadium.*
- *The first game in Texas Stadium was played on October 24, 1971. The Cowboys beat the New England Patriots, 44–21.*
- *Tom Landry won his 200th game in Texas Stadium on December 28, 1980.*

Texas Stadium comes alive on game day.
The Cowboys have played here since 1971.

Dressed for Success

The Dallas uniform is silver, blue, and white—with a big Star of Texas on the helmet. The team's uniform has looked this way since the mid 1960s. Before that, the Cowboys uniform was blue and white. It had stars on the shoulders, and on the helmet, too. At times, the Cowboys have worn uniforms that were a combination of the new and old styles.

The Cowboys believe that their white uniforms are lucky, so they wear them whenever possible. NFL rules say that the home team gets to choose its uniform color, so the Cowboys pick white when they play in Texas Stadium. When they play on the road, the team they are facing usually wears its dark colors, so Dallas also wears white. Sometimes, the home team will be sneaky and choose white—forcing the Cowboys to wear their blue jerseys.

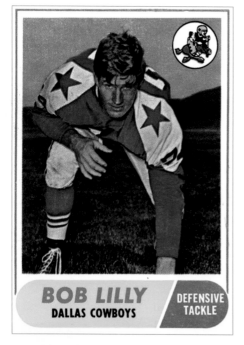

BOB LILLY
DALLAS COWBOYS
DEFENSIVE TACKLE

Bob Lilly shows off the star-studded shoulders of the Cowboys' early uniform.

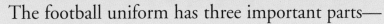

The football uniform has three important parts—

- Helmet
- Jersey
- Pants

Helmets used to be made out of leather, and they did not have facemasks—ouch! Today, helmets are made of super-strong plastic. The uniform top, or jersey, is made of thick fabric. It fits snugly around a player so that tacklers cannot grab it and pull him down. The pants come down just over the knees.

There is a lot more to a football uniform than what you see on the outside. Air can be pumped inside the helmet to give it a snug, padded fit. The jersey covers shoulder pads, and sometimes a rib-protector called a "flak jacket." The pants include pads that protect the hips, thighs, *tailbone*, and knees.

Football teams have two sets of uniforms—one dark and one light. This makes it easier to tell two teams apart on the field.

Marion Barber heads for the end zone wearing the team's modern uniform.

We Won!

The Cowboys won five Super Bowls between 1960 and 2005. Only the San Francisco 49ers have won as many, and no one has won more. The Cowboys played in eight Super Bowls during this time—an all-time record. The three Super Bowls they lost (one to the Baltimore Colts and two to the Pittsburgh Steelers) were exciting right to the very end. With a little luck, the Cowboys could have won all eight!

The Cowboys have always played their best in the most important games. In Super Bowl VI, they beat the Miami Dolphins 24–3. It was the first time ever in a Super Bowl that one team kept another from scoring a touchdown. Quarterback Roger Staubach was named **Most Valuable Player (MVP)** of the game, but even he said that the entire defense deserved the award.

LEFT: Roger Staubach outruns Bill Stanfill of the Dolphins during Super Bowl VI. **RIGHT**: Ed "Too Tall" Jones smashes into Denver quarterback Craig Morton during Super Bowl XXII.

The Dallas defense had another excellent game against the Denver Broncos in Super Bowl XII. They had four interceptions and caused four **fumbles**, and won 27–10. This time two defensive players shared the MVP award—Randy White and Harvey Martin.

The Cowboys' offense was the big story in the Super Bowls of the 1990s. Dallas beat the Buffalo Bills 52–17 in Super Bowl XXVII. It was a true team effort. The defense forced nine turnovers during the game, Troy Aikman passed for four touchdowns, and Emmitt Smith ran for 109 yards.

The Cowboys faced the Bills a year later in Super Bowl XXVIII. Buffalo played well in the first half, and led Dallas 13–6. In the third quarter, Leon Lett of the Cowboys caused a fumble and James Washington ran the ball into the end zone to tie the score. From that point on, the game belonged to Aikman and Smith. The Cowboys scored two more touchdowns and a field goal to win 30–13.

Two years later, the Cowboys played in their eighth Super Bowl. They defeated the Pittsburgh Steelers 27–17. The difference in the game was two interceptions by defensive back Larry Brown. Each led to a touchdown in the second half. This victory was extra-sweet for Dallas fans. The Steelers had beaten the Cowboys in two Super Bowls during the 1970s. It took more than 15 years, but they finally had their *revenge*.

ABOVE: Troy Aikman shakes Emmitt Smith's hand after a touchdown.
LEFT: Larry Brown looks for running room after one of his interceptions in Super Bowl XXX.

Go-To Guys

To be a true star in the NFL, you need more than fast feet and a big body. You have to be a "go-to guy"—someone the coach wants on the field at the end of a big game. Cowboys fans have had a lot to cheer about over the years, including these great stars…

THE PIONEERS

DON MEREDITH   Quarterback

• BORN: 4/10/1938   • PLAYED FOR TEAM: 1960 TO 1968

Don Meredith was the Cowboys' first great quarterback. "Dandy Don" loved to have fun while he played. He could make just about anyone laugh, except his super-serious coach, Tom Landry.

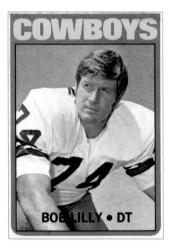

BOB LILLY   Defensive Lineman

• BORN: 7/26/1939   • PLAYED FOR TEAM: 1961 TO 1974

Bob Lilly was the best tackler on the Cowboys in the 1960s and 1970s. He was so hard to run away from that many teams ran their plays right *at* him. Lilly may have been the best defensive tackle the NFL has ever seen.

MEL RENFRO   Defensive Back

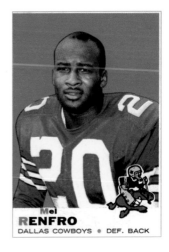

• BORN: 12/30/1941   • PLAYED FOR TEAM: 1964 TO 1977

Mel Renfro was the man who stopped other teams from passing against the Cowboys. He played safety and cornerback, and was a star at both positions. Renfro was chosen to play in the **Pro Bowl** in each of his first 10 NFL seasons.

ROGER STAUBACH   Quarterback

• BORN: 2/5/1942   • PLAYED FOR TEAM: 1969 TO 1979

Roger Staubach could win with his passing or his running—he was great at both. No matter how far behind the Cowboys were, he never gave up. In all, he led the team back from the edge of defeat to thrilling victories 23 times.

RANDY WHITE   Defensive Lineman

• BORN: 1/15/1953   • PLAYED FOR TEAM: 1975 TO 1988

Randy White went from his **three-point stance** to full speed faster than any lineman in the NFL. He was voted the best at his position eight years in a row. Someone once said that White was half-man and half-monster. From that day on, his nickname was "Man-ster."

LEFT: Bob Lilly   **ABOVE**: Mel Renfro   **RIGHT**: Randy White

JAY NOVACEK   Tight End

• BORN: 10/24/1962   • PLAYED FOR TEAM: 1990 TO 1995

Jay Novacek was everything a team looks for in a tight end. He was big and fast, with **soft hands** and quick feet. No one was better at finding ways to get open, and few players worked harder on blocking.

MICHAEL IRVIN   Receiver

• BORN: 3/5/1966

• PLAYED FOR TEAM: 1988 TO 1999

Michael Irvin was tall, fast, and fearless. For him, catching a pass and getting crushed by two or three tacklers was like a badge of honor. In 1995, he gained 100 or more receiving yards in 11 games in a row.

TROY AIKMAN   Quarterback

• BORN: 11/21/1966   • PLAYED FOR TEAM: 1989 TO 2000

Troy Aikman led the Cowboys to three Super Bowls in the 1990s. He was a sharp, accurate passer who loved to win. Aikman could have thrown more touchdown passes with a different NFL team, but he was more interested in the final score than his own statistics.

ABOVE: Michael Irvin.   **TOP RIGHT**: Larry Allen
BOTTOM RIGHT: Roy Williams

EMMITT SMITH Running Back

- BORN: 5/15/1969 • PLAYED FOR TEAM: 1990 TO 2002

At 5' 9", Emmitt Smith was a "little man" in the world of the NFL. When he ran the football, however, no one was "bigger." Smith gained 1,000 or more yards 11 years in a row for the Cowboys and led the NFL in touchdowns three times. He retired as the league's all-time leading **rusher**.

LARRY ALLEN Guard

- BORN: 11/27/1971

- FIRST SEASON WITH TEAM: 1994

Larry Allen made a name for himself by flattening defensive players. Though he weighed more than 300 pounds, he was amazingly quick and *nimble*. Allen has been voted to the Pro Bowl more than any other player in team history.

ROY WILLIAMS Defensive Back

- BORN: 8/14/1980

- FIRST SEASON WITH TEAM: 2002

Roy Williams became the hardest-hitting safety in the NFL after joining Dallas in 2002. He was fast enough to cover the quickest receivers, and strong enough to tackle the biggest runners.

On the Sidelines

The man on the sidelines for most of the Cowboys' history was Tom Landry. He coached Dallas from 1960 to 1988, and built a very exciting team.

When the Cowboys had the ball, they ran a different play from a different **formation** almost every time. No one knew what they would do next. When the other team had the ball, the Cowboys used a special "Flex" defense. This was hard for quarterbacks to figure out, which made scoring a touchdown against Dallas almost impossible. Under Landry, the Cowboys won 250 regular season games and 20 **postseason** games.

After Landry retired, Jimmy Johnson took over as coach. Johnson helped the Cowboys return to the Super Bowl. He was an old friend of the team's new owner, Jerry Jones. Later, Jones hired other top coaches, including Barry Switzer and Bill Parcells. Switzer was a famous college coach. He won a Super Bowl in his second year with the Cowboys. Parcells led both the New York Giants and New England Patriots to the Super Bowl. He was hired in 2003 to rebuild Dallas into a championship team.

Bill Parcells watches the Cowboys practice.
He was one of several top coaches hired by team owner Jerry Jones.

One Great Day

The Cowboys and Minnesota Vikings were two of the best teams in football during the 1975 season. When they met in the playoffs that winter, everyone knew it would be a great game. Both teams played tough defense. Both teams had good, smart quarterbacks.

WIDE RECEIVER
DREW PEARSON

Drew Pearson

Roger Staubach was the man in charge for the Cowboys. Fran Tarkenton was the leader of the Vikings. They were chased by tacklers all day. Neither quarterback could take control of the game until the end of the fourth quarter. Finally, Tarkenton led the Vikings on a long touchdown **drive** and they went ahead 14–10.

Staubach got the ball on his own 15 yard line with less than two minutes left. The Vikings' defense would not let him move the Cowboys past **midfield**. With time left for just one more play, Staubach threw the

Paul Krause leaps over teammate Nate Wright, but it is too late to catch Drew Pearson, who is just a few feet away from the goal line.

ball as high and as far as he could and "prayed" for the best.

His favorite receiver, Drew Pearson, saw that the pass would not reach the end zone. He bumped one Viking defender, **darted** in front of another, caught the ball, and crossed the goal line for the winning touchdown. To this day, Dallas fans call Staubach's amazing pass the "Hail Mary" after a popular prayer.

Legend Has It

Did the Cowboys really have a "two-headed" quarterback?

LEGEND HAS IT that they did—twice! In 1963, coach Tom Landry had Eddie LeBaron and Don Meredith take turns on each down. One would jog to the sideline, while the other would join the huddle and call Landry's new play. How did their teammates remember who was in the game? One way was by their height. Meredith stood six feet three inches and LeBaron was only five feet eight inches.

Roger Staubach and Craig Morton flank coach Tom Landry.

In 1971, Landry did the same thing with Craig Morton and Roger Staubach. None of these players actually had two heads, of course, but their teammates often had to look into their helmets to make sure they knew who was in the game.

Was Bob Hayes the fastest receiver ever to play in the NFL?

LEGEND HAS IT that he was. In fact, when he joined the Cowboys in 1965, Hayes was the world's fastest human. He was the first person to run the 60-yard dash in 6.0 seconds, and the first to run the 100-yard dash in 9.1 seconds. Hayes won two gold medals in the 1964 **Summer Olympics**, then led the NFL with 12 touchdowns in 1965. He caught 371 passes and scored 76 touchdowns during his 11-year career.

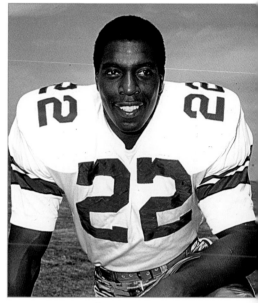

Bob Hayes

How did the Cowboys' famous "Doomsday Defense" get its nickname?

LEGEND HAS IT that the Cowboys just wanted a cool nickname like everyone else. The Los Angeles Rams had the "Fearsome Foursome." The Minnesota Vikings had the "Purple People Eaters." In 1966, someone came up with "Doomsday Defense" and it stuck. Forty years later, Cowboy fans still loved the nickname.

It Really Happened

O ne of the greatest honors a football player can receive is the MVP trophy from the Super Bowl. It means that you were the most valuable player on the world's best team that day. At least, it usually does.

On January 17, 1971, the Dallas Cowboys played the Baltimore Colts in Super Bowl V. Some of the best players in the NFL were on the field that day, but you would not have known it from the

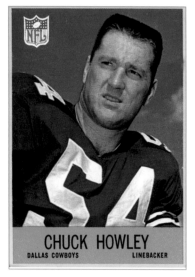

CHUCK HOWLEY
DALLAS COWBOYS   LINEBACKER

way they played. The Colts and Cowboys had so many fumbles and interceptions that fans called this game the "Blooper Bowl."

One player stood out from all the others in Super Bowl V. His name was Chuck Howley, and he played linebacker for the Cowboys. He was an "old-timer" who had been in the NFL since the 1950s. But against the Colts, he played like a young man. Howley seemed to be everywhere at once. He was making tackles, rushing the quarterback, defending passes, and creating all kinds of problems for the Colts.

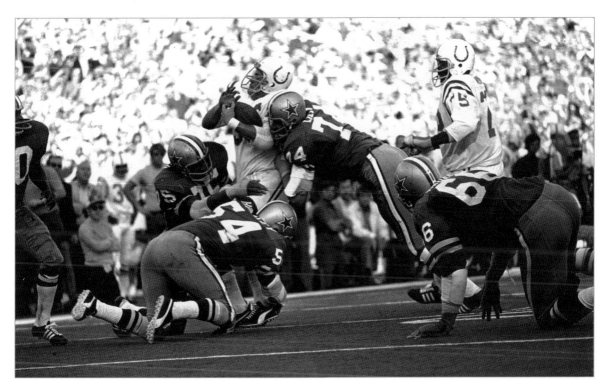

Howley intercepted passes twice to stop Baltimore drives, but Colts' defense was just as tough. The score was tied 13–13 late in the fourth quarter when the Cowboys made one last mistake. The Colts intercepted a pass, and then kicked a **field goal** to win. When the MVP voters had to pick the game's best players, there was no question that it should be Chuck Howley—even though his team lost.

Bruised, battered, and exhausted, Howley was grateful when the MVP trophy was given to him in the Cowboys' locker room, but still sad his team had lost. "The award is tremendous," he told reporters. "But I wish it were the world championship. They go hand in hand."

TOP: Chuck Howley makes a low tackle with the help of teammates Jethro Pugh and Bob Lilly in Super Bowl V. **LEFT**: Chuck Howley

Team Spirit

In most NFL stadiums, team spirit can be measured in noise. When the Cowboys play at home, team spirit can also be measured in warmth. No football team has a closer relationship with its fans. They support the Cowboys 365 days a year, and make the players feel like part of one big, happy family.

The players love being part of this community. Many remain in Dallas after they retire. Whether they were big stars or **bench-warmers**, they know that the city is a place they can always call "home."

Dallas is also home to football's most famous cheerleaders. In 1976, the Cowboys decided to make their cheerleading squad into a professional dance team. The Dallas Cowboys Cheerleaders soon became almost as famous as the Cowboys. After seeing how much the fans loved it, many NFL teams copied this idea.

The Dallas Cowboys Cheerleaders were football's first professional dance team.

Timeline

In this timeline, each Super Bowl is listed under the year it was played. Remember that the Super Bowl is held early in the year, and is actually part of the previous season. For example, Super Bowl XL was played on February 4 of 2006, but it was the championship of the 2005 NFL season.

1966
Don Meredith quarterbacks the Cowboys to their first winning season.

1972
The Cowboys beat the Miami Dolphins in Super Bowl VI, 24–3.

1960
The Cowboys join the NFL.

1965
Bob Hayes leads the NFL in touchdowns.

1971
The team moves from the Cotton Bowl to Texas Stadium.

Eddie LeBaron, quarterback of the 1960 Cowboys.

EDDIE LE BARON
QUARTERBACK   DALLAS COWBOYS

Bob Hayes

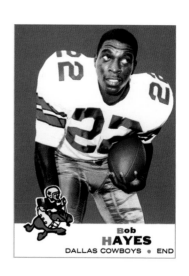

Bob
HAYES
DALLAS COWBOYS ● END

1978
The Cowboys defeat the Denver Broncos in Super Bowl XII.

Larry Brown accepts his Super Bowl MVP award in 1996.

1988
Tom Landry coaches his 29th and final season.

1996
The Cowboys win Super Bowl XXX.

1993
The Cowboys defeat the Buffalo Bills 52–17 in Super Bowl XXVII.

1994
The Cowboys win Super Bowl XXVIII.

2001
Emmitt Smith rushes for 1,000 yards for the 11th year in a row.

Troy Aikman, MVP of Super Bowl XXVII.

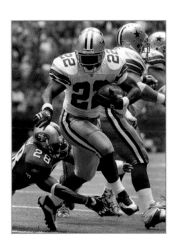

Emmitt Smith

Fun Facts

RUNNING THE NUMBERS

The Cowboys were the first NFL team to use a computer to predict how young players would do in the NFL.

RUN, TONY, RUN!

Tony Dorsett once made a 99-yard touchdown run against the Minnesota Vikings. It is still the longest in NFL history.

TAKE THE WHEEL

Defensive stars Randy White and Harvey Martin were named Co-MVPs of Super Bowl XII. Their teammates joked that they were the only two players strong enough to "split" the prize—a new car.

Randy White and Harvey Martin team up on a tackle.

GLUED TO THE TUBE

More than 102 million TV viewers saw the Cowboys win Super Bowl XII in January of 1978. It was the first time that more than 100 million people had ever watched a football game.

GET BACK IN THERE

The Cowboys have had some famous **two-way players**. Danny White was their **punter** and quarterback during the 1980s. Deion Sanders played offense and defense for Dallas in the Super Bowl.

Deion Sanders

ONE OF THE 'BOYS

Jerry Jones, who bought the Cowboys in 1989, never liked to sit in the owner's "luxury box" during games. He preferred to stand with the players on the sidelines.

LET'S MAKE A DEAL

In 1989, the Cowboys and Minnesota Vikings made the NFL's biggest trade ever. A total of 18 players were swapped.

Talking Football

Emmitt Smith

"They can't measure the size of a player's heart...and that's what they left out of my scouting report."

—Emmitt Smith, on being called "too small" to make it in the NFL

"I love to play football. I love the competition. I love the atmosphere—from the locker room to the games."

—Troy Aikman, on being a Cowboy

"Our goal was to stop the run and force teams into passing situations. It worked pretty well. Someone would run on us maybe one game in a season."

—Bob Lilly, on the "Doomsday Defense" of the 1960s and 1970s

Tom Landry

"I had the great fortune of coaching many great players in my career."
— *Tom Landry, on the many stars who played for him*

"If a kid loses, he shouldn't worry about it, but should
learn from the experience…at the professional level,
there is no substitute for winning."
— *Roger Staubach, on winning and losing*

"You may be the best in the game—and you may even
believe it—but you can't sit back and relax.
You've got to be constantly working to get better."
— *Randy White, on the first rule of being a Cowboy*

For the Record

The great Cowboy teams and players have left their marks on the record books. These are the "best of the best"…

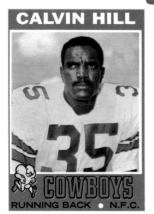

Calvin Hill

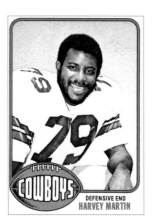

Harvey Martin

COWBOYS AWARD WINNERS

WINNER	AWARD	YEAR
Tom Landry	NFL Coach of the Year	1966
Calvin Hill	Rookie of the Year*	1969
Chuck Howley	Super Bowl V MVP	1971
Roger Staubach	Super Bowl VI MVP	1972
Tom Landry	NFL Coach of the Year	1975
Tony Dorsett	Rookie of the Year	1977
Harvey Martin	Defensive Player of the Year	1977
Harvey Martin	Super Bowl XII Co-MVP	1978
Randy White	Super Bowl XII Co-MVP	1978
Jimmy Johnson	NFC Coach of the Year	1990
Troy Aikman	Super Bowl XXVII MVP	1993
Emmitt Smith	Most Valuable Player	1993
Emmitt Smith	Super Bowl XXVIII MVP	1994
Larry Brown	Super Bowl XXX MVP	1996

An award given to the league's best first-year player.

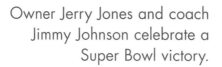

Owner Jerry Jones and coach Jimmy Johnson celebrate a Super Bowl victory.

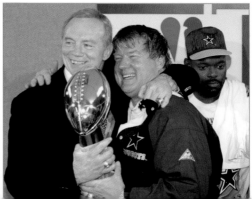

COWBOYS ACHIEVEMENTS

ACHIEVEMENT	YEAR
NFC Champions	1970
NFC Champions	1971
Super Bowl VI Champions	1971*
NFC Champions	1975
NFC Champions	1977
Super Bowl XII Champions	1977*
NFC Champions	1978
NFC Champions	1992
Super Bowl XXVII Champions	1992*
NFC Champions	1993
Super Bowl XXVIII Champions	1993*
NFC Champions	1995
Super Bowl XXX Champions	1995*

Super Bowls are played early the following year, but the game is counted as the championship of this season.

ABOVE: Tony Dorsett
BOTTOM: Tom Landry is carried off the field after winning Super Bowl XII.

Pinpoints

The history of a football team is made up of many smaller stories. These stories take place all over the map—not just in the city a team calls "home." Match the push-pins on these maps to the Team Facts and you will begin to see the story of the Cowboys unfold!

TEAM FACTS

1 Dallas, Texas—*The Cowboys have played in this area since 1960.*

2 West Covina, California—*Troy Aikman was born here.*

3 Mission, Texas—*Tom Landry was born here.*

4 New Orleans, Louisiana—*The Cowboys won two Super Bowls here.*

5 Mobile, Alabama—*Leon Lett was born here.*

6 Pensacola, Florida—*Emmitt Smith was born here.*

7 Baltimore, Maryland—*Calvin Hill was born here.*

8 South River, New Jersey—*Drew Pearson was born here.*

9 Rochester, Pennsylvania—*Tony Dorsett was born here.*

10 Cincinnati, Ohio—*Roger Staubach was born here.*

11 Guadalajara, Mexico—*Efren Herrera was born here.*

12 East Brighton, Australia—*Punter Mat McBriar was born here.*

Efren Herrera, who led the team in points in 1976 and 1977.

Play Ball

Football is a sport played by two teams on a field that is 100 yards long. The game is divided into four 15-minute quarters. Each team must have 11 players on the field at all times. The group that has the ball is called the offense. The group trying to keep the offense from moving the ball forward is called the defense.

A football game is made up of a series of "plays." Each play starts and ends with a referee's signal. A play begins when the center snaps the ball between his legs to the quarterback. The quarterback then gives the ball to a teammate, throws (or "passes") the ball to a teammate, or runs with the ball himself. The job of the defense is to tackle the player with the ball or stop the quarterback's pass. A play ends when the ball (or player holding the ball) is "down." The offense must move the ball forward at least 10 yards every four downs. If it fails to do so, the other team is given the ball. If the offense has not made 10 yards after three downs—and does not want to risk losing the ball—it can kick (or "punt") the ball to make the other team start from its own end of the field.

At each end of a football field is a goal line, which divides the field from the end zone. A team must run or pass the ball over the goal line to score a touchdown, which counts for six points. After scoring a touchdown, a team can try a short kick for one "extra point," or try again to run or pass across the goal line for two points. Teams can score three points from anywhere on the field by kicking the ball between the goal posts. This is called a field goal.

The defense can score two points if it tackles a player while he is in his own end zone. This is called a safety. The defense can also score points by taking the ball away from the offense and crossing the opposite goal line for a touchdown. The team with the most points after 60 minutes is the winner.

Football may seem like a very hard game to understand, but the more you play and watch football, the more "little things" you are likely to notice. The next time you are at a game, look for these plays:

PLAY LIST

BLITZ—A play where the defense sends extra tacklers after the quarterback. If the quarterback sees a blitz coming, he passes the ball quickly. If he does not, he can end up on the bottom of a very big pile!

DRAW—A play where the offense pretends it will pass the ball, and then gives it to a running back. If the offense can "draw" the defense to the quarterback and his receivers, the running back should have lots of room to run.

FLY PATTERN—A play where a team's fastest receiver is told to "fly" past the defensive backs for a long pass. Many long touchdowns are scored on this play.

SQUIB KICK—A play where the ball is kicked a short distance on purpose. A squib kick is used when the team kicking off does not want the other team's fastest player to catch the ball and run with it.

SWEEP—A play where the ball-carrier follows a group of teammates moving sideways to "sweep" the defense out of the way. A good sweep gives the runner a chance to gain a lot of yards before he is tackled or forced out of bounds.

Glossary

FOOTBALL WORDS TO KNOW

AMERICAN FOOTBALL LEAGUE (AFL)—The football league that began play in 1960, and later merged with the National Football League.

BENCH-WARMER—A player who spends most of the game sitting on the sidelines, where he "warms the bench."

COMPLETE—Throw a pass that is caught.

DRAFT PICKS—College players selected by NFL teams each spring.

DRIVE—A series of plays that drives the defense back toward its own goal.

FIELD GOAL—A goal from the field, kicked over the crossbar and between the goal posts. A field goal is worth three points.

FORMATION—The arrangement of players on the field at the beginning of each play.

FUMBLES—Balls that are dropped by the players carrying them.

HUDDLE—The gathering of players where each new play is called.

INTERCEPTING—Catching a pass meant for an opponent.

MIDFIELD—The 50 yard line.

MOST VALUABLE PLAYER (MVP)—The award given each year to the best player; also given to the best player in the Super Bowl.

NATIONAL FOOTBALL LEAGUE (NFL)—The league that started in 1920 and is still operating today.

NFL CHAMPIONSHIP—The game played each year to decide the winner of the league, from 1933 to 1969.

PRO BOWL—The NFL's all-star game, played after the Super Bowl.

PROFESSIONAL FOOTBALL—Football played for money; college and high-school football is considered amateur football.

POSTSEASON—The games played after the regular season to decide the season champion.

PUNTER—The player who kicks the ball to the other team after his team fails to make a first down.

RUSHER—A player who runs with the football.

SACKING—Tackling the quarterback.

SOFT HANDS—Flexible hands and fingers that make it easier to catch hard passes.

SUMMER OLYMPICS—The international sports competition held every four years.

SUPER BOWL—The championship game of football, played between the winner of the American Football Conference (AFC) and National Football Conference (NFC).

THREE-POINT STANCE—A lineman's crouch, with one hand touching the ground for balance.

TWO-WAY PLAYERS—People who are on the field for both offense and defense for their team.

OTHER WORDS TO KNOW

ASSEMBLE—Put together.

DARTED—Moved quickly and suddenly.

DECADE—A period of 10 years.

DYNASTY—A line of rulers from the same group or family.

NIMBLE—Moving quickly and lightly.

REVENGE—Something done to get back at, or get even with, someone.

TAILBONE—The bone that protects the base of the spine.

TRADITIONS—Beliefs or customs that are handed down from generation to generation.

VETERANS—People who have experience doing a job.

Places to Go

ON THE ROAD

TEXAS STADIUM
2401 East Airport Freeway
Irving, Texas 75062
(972) 556-9900

THE PRO FOOTBALL HALL OF FAME
2121 George Halas Drive NW
Canton, Ohio 44708
(330) 456-8207

ON THE WEB

THE NATIONAL FOOTBALL LEAGUE   www.nfl.com
  • *Learn more about the National Football League*

THE DALLAS COWBOYS   www.Cowboys.com
  • *Learn more about the Dallas Cowboys*

THE PRO FOOTBALL HALL OF FAME   www.profootballhof.com
  • *Learn more about football's greatest players*

ON THE BOOKSHELF

To learn more about the sport of football, look for these books at your library or bookstore:

  • Ingram, Scott. *A Football All-Pro*. Chicago, IL.: Heinemann Library, 2005.
  • Kennedy, Mike. *Football*. Danbury, CT.: Franklin Watts, 2003.
  • Suen, Anastasia. *The Story of Football*. New York, NY.: PowerKids Press, 2002.

Index

PAGE NUMBERS IN **BOLD** REFER TO ILLUSTRATIONS.

The Team

MARK STEWART has written more than 20 books on football, and over 100 sports books for kids. He grew up in New York City during the 1960s rooting for the Giants and Jets, and now takes his two daughters, Mariah and Rachel, to watch them play in their home state of New Jersey. Mark comes from a family of writers. His grandfather was Sunday Editor of *The New York Times* and his mother was Articles Editor of *The Ladies Home Journal* and *McCall's*. Mark has profiled hundreds of athletes over the last 20 years. He has also written several books about New York and New Jersey. Mark is a graduate of Duke University, with a degree in history. He lives with his daughters and wife, Sarah, overlooking Sandy Hook, NJ.

JASON AIKENS is the Collections Curator at the Pro Football Hall of Fame. He is responsible for the preservation of the Pro Football Hall of Fame's collection of artifacts and memorabilia and obtaining new donations of memorabilia from current players and NFL teams. Jason has a Bachelor of Arts in History from Michigan State University and a Masters in History from Western Michigan University where he concentrated on sports history. Jason has been working for the Pro Football Hall of Fame since 1997; before that he was an intern at the College Football Hall of Fame. Jason's family has roots in California and has been following the St. Louis Rams since their days in Los Angeles, California. He lives with his wife Cynthia in Canton, OH.